The Boy Who Dreamed To Be With His Parents On Saipan!

Riza Oledan-Ramos

Illustrated by: Rodante Guarda
Edited by: Heather Linday
Design & Layout: Walt F.J. Goodridge

Published by:
Riza Ramos Books, Saipan, USA

The Boy Who Dreamed to Be With His Parents on Saipan!

Published and distributed by:
Riza Ramos Books
PMB 3372 PO BOX 10002
Saipan, MP 96950
email: riza@rizaramosbooks.com

Inquiries to the author may be addressed to:
Riza Ramos
PMB 3372 PO BOX 10002
Saipan, MP 96950
email: riza@rizaramosbooks.com

Back cover photo by Nelson Pagaduan
Sign up to Riza's mailing list at www.rizaramosbooks.com

Educational institutions, government agencies, libraries and corporations are invited to inquire about quantity discounts.

Retail Cost: $14.95
ISBN-10: 0-9828684-0-5   ISBN-13: 978-0-9828684-0-9

Printed in the United States of America   First Edition

CONTENTS

For all children who, like me, wish to be together with both their mom and dad.

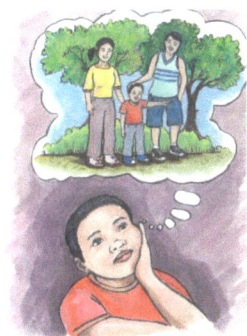

Chapter 1
Me

On December 25, 2000, at 6:40 pm, while the choirs were busy singing their caroling songs in the Philippines, my first cry was also heard.

My mom tells me that all babies cry, but I think I was crying because I was sad. I was sad because my dad wasn't there when my mom gave birth to me.

Mom said I was very small when I was born, and that I weighed only 4.8 pounds! Even though I was small, I grew up very fast!

My dad was working as a construction man on the island of Saipan. He wasn't able to come home because his salary was delayed, so he didn't have enough money to buy the airplane ticket.

Since my dad wasn't there, my Grandma Cenia, Grandpa Salvador and Aunt Socorro were there to take care of me and my mom instead.

7

Mom named me Emmanuel because my birthday was on Christmas day. My name means "God with us."

Mom tells me that she didn't prepare a boy's name because she thought I was a girl when I was still in her tummy. If I turned out to be a girl, mom said my name was going to be Fiona Riza. That's a nice name, but I'm glad she didn't name me Fiona! I am a boy! I am a boy with a single great dream. I am a boy who dreamed to be with his parents on Saipan!

Chapter 2
My Long Distance Family

Do you know what a "long distance family" is? My childhood years seem to be what grown-ups call a "long distance relationship." Because I've almost always been a long distance away from both my mom and dad, I call our family a long distance family. When you grow up in a long distance family, you don't get to be with your mom and dad as much as you want to.

Dad wasn't there when I had my baptism. Dad wasn't there when I blew out my first birthday candle. No matter how much he wanted to be with me, my dad didn't have a chance because there just wasn't enough money.

The construction company he had been working for on Saipan closed its doors leaving my dad and his co-workers jobless. They survived with the help of friends and the assistance they got from KARIDAT (an organization that helps people in need).

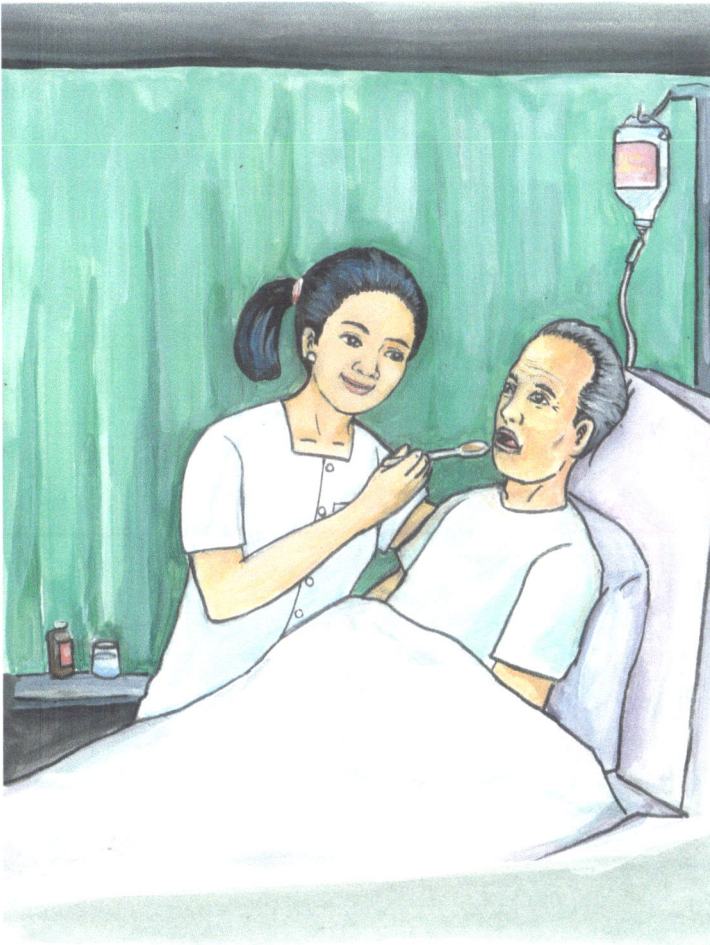

Then, when I was about one year old, my mom, too, decided to go back to work. She said she needed to have a job to support me. So, my mom started working in a hospital about an hour ride from our house. My mom is a nurse.

I was very small, but I remember that sometimes I didn't see my mom during the day, and sometimes I didn't see her during the night. I learned from my mom that a nurse has to work in the daytime, and at night time, too, because sick people need to be looked after day and night.

For as long as I can remember, I've always had a big dream that we could stop being a long distance family, and that I could have them by my side all the time.

I was not the only one in my family who had a big dream. Mom also had a dream—a dream to be together with my dad and with me as one big happy family.

When mom was away at her job, she left me with my Aunt Socorro, and Grandma Cenia. My cousins, Faye and Shayne, Aunt Socorro's daughters, also looked after me.

Every morning, when Grandpa Salvador went to his small farm, I went with him too. I enjoyed feeding his cow while running around the field.

In the Philippines, we have water buffalos called carabaos that farmers like my grandpa use to help plow their fields. It was lots of fun when grandpa allowed me to ride his carabao. I also enjoyed catching grasshoppers and dragonflies. What I enjoyed most was seeing the tadpoles and the cute little frogs in the rice field.

I often played with my friends, Jayson and Cedrick. Their parents were also working in far-away places. But whatever I did, and however much fun I had, I was always eager to see my mom when she came home from work. I was always excited to open her bag, because I was sure there was always something in there that she brought for me!

Chapter 3
The First Time I Saw My Dad

I was about one year and seven months old when the dad I saw in pictures, the dad I heard over the phone, and the dad I had only seen in my dreams, finally came to me in real life!

He had found a new, good-paying job on Saipan, and was able to save money for his vacation.

I was a little shy the first time I saw my dad, but we soon got along very well together. I loved to be with my dad and played with him all day long. I learned for the first time that even though I had a mom, aunties, cousins and grandparents, it was good to have a dad, too!

While dad was visiting, we went to some beautiful places, like the beach and waterfall in my mom's hometown in the Philippines. We also stayed for almost a whole month in Manila with my dad's parents, Grandpa Diego and Grandma Lina.

17

After only a month, dad went back to Saipan. He said he needed to go back to work so that he could send us money.

I felt so sad, but dad left with a promise for me. He promised that someday I would go to Saipan, and that the three of us would be together.

That was the day my dream was born—the dream to be with my parents on Saipan. I imagined that one day we would walk in the park holding hands as a family. The moment I learned to draw, even before I started school, I already had a favorite drawing. It was a picture of three people walking together holding hands. It was our family.

Whenever mom sent letters to dad, she would send him my drawings too.

Every time my dad called us on the phone from Saipan, I always reminded him about his promise and my big dream. I believed my dad would keep his promise, and that my dream would come true, just as my mom always told me dreams could.

Chapter 4
My First Days in School

My mom wasn't there to take care of me or to pack my lunch for my first days in kindergarten in my mom's hometown. She had gone to the city of Manila, in the Philippines, to train in a big kidney hospital. She said she needed the training before she could go to be with my dad and work in Saipan, too.

It was my Aunt Socorro who prepared my school supplies and my uniform.

It was Aunt Socorro who walked with me to school. Even though Aunt Socorro took good care of me, I would envy those kids who were picked by their real mom or dad after school.

Mom and dad often called me and sent me money and toys, but sometimes I felt that I didn't need any of these things at all. What I really needed was them.

23

Day after day, I kept wishing that the time would come when the three of us would finally be together. It was my only wish every time I blew out my birthday candles. I wished that the big dream in my drawing would come true.

Aunt Socorro was so kind. She was always there to take care of me. I became close to her, and, in fact, I called her "mom" too. She said that even though she didn't have the chance to have a son, she had been blessed with the chance to care of me. She said it was like having a son of her own.

Mom finally came home after six months of training in Manila. I thought she would finally stay with me for good, but she left again after just a month. She said she already got a new job in Manila, and that she needed the job experience at this new job before she could go to be with my dad. Although it made me sad, mom told me that she was doing it for my best.

During the Thanksgiving mass on my Kindergarten graduation day, I almost cried when I thought about my mom not being able to see me graduate. Only Aunt Socorro would be able to attend. I told Aunt Socorro that I would never talk to my mom again if she didn't come.

But, mom was able to make it! She said she took the last flight from Manila just to be there with me!

Mom really loves me and I really knew it on this day! It made me so happy to have her home!

However, mom had come home just to attend my graduation. She had to go back to Manila right away for her job.

Before she left, however, she gave me a very special graduation present. She told me that she would be going to Saipan to be with dad soon, and that I'd be going with her too!

Although it made me sad to see her leave again, there was now a new joy in my thoughts that at last my dream—my big dream—would soon come true!

CHAPTER 5
On My Way to Manila

One day, Aunt Socorro told me she was going to Manila. Her daughters, Faye and Shayne—my cousins—were both going to college. I got excited when I found out I was going too! I was going to Manila, the city where my mom and dad met when my mom was studying at college. I would finally be in the same city where mom was working!

When grandma Cenia and Grandpa Salvador learned about this, they became sad. Grandpa Salvador told me he and grandma were going to be like newlyweds, because only the two of them would be left in the house.

Even though he was sad, Grandpa Salvador told me that it is normal for children to leave their parents when the children become grown-ups.

A day before we left for Manila, Grandpa Salvador took me to his farm to say goodbye to his cow and carabao. I'm sure I'm going to miss feeding them, just like I will miss Cedrick and Jason, my two friends.

Aunt Socorro told my grandparents that we would visit them every now and then. My grandparents said, "It's okay," but I knew they were sad.

CHAPTER 6
School Days in Manila

My cousins, Faye and Shayne, enrolled in universities while my mom enrolled me in Fidelis Children's Academy in Manila, Philippines. Fidelis was just a few blocks from our rented apartment. We lived happily together with my aunt Socorro, my mom and my cousins Faye and Shayne.

I liked going to Fidelis, especially when my mom would have a day off from work.

On those days, she would meet me at my school at lunchtime, and treat me for a hamburger at a burger house that was just a few steps away from our school. I finally felt just like the other kids whose parents were there for them!

31

Sometimes on Sundays we went to the mall to watch movies, or to dinner with my cousins and Aunt Socorro. We also went to the zoo. I saw monkeys, tigers, and different kinds of fish, but what attracted me the most was a cute baby gorilla wearing diapers!

Dad's parents also lived in Manila. So, on Sundays, I stayed with dad's parents, Grandpa Diego and Grandma Lina. I enjoyed playing with my cousins Louie and Limuel.

I loved being together with my mom in Manila! It made me happy to be with her, but deep inside I still had this dream, a dream to be with my dad, too!

Then one day my mom told me that she was leaving again to go to Saipan. She had waited years for her job application at a hospital on Saipan to be approved, and it finally came through.

However, when I found out that mom was going alone, I cried and cried. I thought she had made a promise that when she went to Saipan, that I would go with her. I was so very sad.

With tears in my eyes, I asked my mom why she had to leave me again to work. When she said she was doing it for me, it felt like she was not answering my question. It was for my best, she said, the same words she always tells me every time she leaves me.

"Mom, how could it be for my best when you have to leave me?" I asked her again.

But mom didn't answer me. She simply said someday I'll understand. But, I wish my mom and dad didn't have to leave me to work.

My Aunt Socorro told me she would always be there to take care of me as she always did whenever my mom left. My cousins, Faye and Shayne, also told me that everything was going to be all right.

I wasn't the only one with a long distance family. Uncle Felimon, Faye's and Shayne's dad, wasn't always with them either. He works in a ship, a big, big, ship very far away. Uncle Felimon also plays with me when he's home.

Even my mom's brother, Uncle Edgar, is also away from my cousin Jasper and Aunt Len. Mom said Uncle Edgar is a brilliant Mechanical Engineer, but he chose to work abroad for his family's best.

While mom was away, Aunt Socorro took care of me. Mom and dad called me every week, and kept telling me that soon I was going to be with them in Saipan.

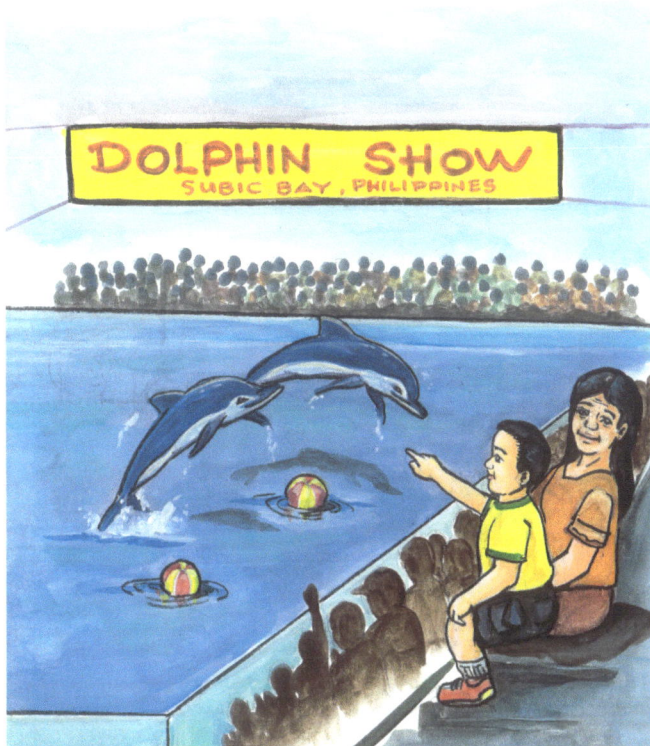

It was Aunt Socorro who attended all my school affairs, like the field trip we had to Subic Bay, Philippines, where we watched the dolphin show.

Subic Bay is a three-hour ride by bus from Manila. It's a very nice, clean city where you can see monkeys on the road.

It was Aunt Socorro and my cousins Faye and Shayne who attended my Recognition Day. Even my dad's parents were not there because Grandma Lina was sick.

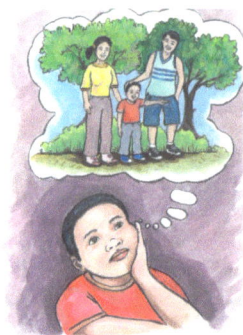

CHAPTER 7
On My Way to Saipan

After one whole year at school, hoping that mom would come home to take me to Saipan, she came back! She told me I would be going with her to Saipan!

I was so happy, but when I looked at Aunt Socorro, her face was so sad. Aunt Socorro is like a mom to me now, too. She cooks my favorite dish—adobo. She washes my clothes. She makes me happy when I'm sad. She buys my favorite toys. She brings me to the doctor when I'm sick, and most of all she treats me like her own son. I felt she would be sad when I left to be with my mom and dad on Saipan.

My cousins seemed sad too, they were like my sisters, and have looked after me since I was a baby.

As I said goodbye to everyone, I told them I would call very often so they would not be lonely. I also asked Aunt Socorro to visit us someday in Saipan.

Mom and I then went to the airport.

39

As we flew on the airplane, Mom told me all about Saipan. Mom said that Saipan is a beautiful island and a nice place to live, with nice people too.

Mom also told me that Saipan is like a paradise! Saipan has nice weather, white sandy beaches, fresh, clean air, many trees, delicious fruits and beautiful surroundings.

I was very excited to see Saipan, and really excited to finally see my dad, too! I wondered how my dad looked now.

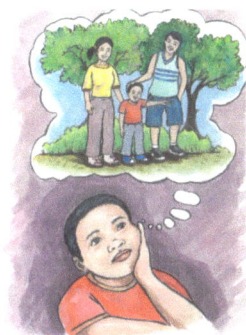

CHAPTER 8
A Dream Come True

On July 11, 2007, I stepped foot on Saipan for the first time. At last! I was so excited! I was going to be with my dad, and with my mom! All of us would finally be together! We would no longer be a long distance family!

Even though the last time I saw my dad was four years before, I was the first one to recognize him when mom and I came outside of the airport. Dad had always sent us photographs of himself and his coworkers and pictures of Saipan while he had been away from my mom and me.

42

For me, this was a new beginning. At last, the picture in my drawing was happening! Mom was right, Saipan is really a nice island with nice people, too. I'm glad I have the chance to live in this beautiful place. I have enjoyed playing and running on the white sandy beaches with my parents.

*****

On December 25, 2007, I celebrated my seventh birthday—and Christmas—for the first time with my mom and dad! We shouted the New Year countdown to 2008 together on Saipan. It made me so happy!

I told Aunt Socorro back in Manila about it, and she said she was happy for me. She looks forward to visiting us on Saipan someday. Now I'm beginning to understand why mom and dad leave for a job. They wanted to give me all the nice things they could. Mom and dad bought me nice shoes, bags and toys. But, most of all, what makes me the happiest is that mom and dad kept their promise to be with me.

At last my dream has come true!

Now I know that whatever dreams I have from now on, that God is with me, and is always there to help me make my dreams come true!

A Message from the Author:

On August 18, 2009 my third grade son asked me to help him with his school project in Language under Mrs. Frances Taimanao in Mt. Carmel School, Saipan, Commonwealth of the Northern Mariana Islands. However, this was not the usual project or art work like he has had since the first grade, it was his autobiography.

We started collecting his baby pictures and revisited events that had occurred in his life. My son shared his thoughts as we looked the photographs. As I input his words into the computer, he told me things he remembered, things he actually felt, and things that I had missed while I was away from him.

As I typed, I realized that to capture his thoughts accurately, I needed to put myself in his shoes, and think like a child. I asked my son for things I could hardly describe, but he was smart enough to answer me in a child's way. During the process, I felt how sad it is for a child to be left by his/her mom or dad. I imagined how many children are being left by mothers or fathers for a job far from home.

As we finished my son's project, I had an idea that we could actually make a real book; a book worthy enough to share with the world. Every day in the Philippines and around the world many parents are leaving their home country to find work elsewhere to give their children a better future, I for one, am one of these parents. My brother and brother-in-law also work in foreign countries, all with the same motivation: to gain a better life for us and our children.

This is a story not just for Filipino children, but for all children in the world with a mom or dad living far away, who in one way or another have had the same experiences as my son.

This book is not only for kids to enjoy, but also for parents. This is like your child opening his feelings to you. My aim is not only to make reading memorable to children, but also to touch a parents' heart with simple words from a child's points of view.

HAVE FUN READING!

45

Acknowledgements

To the Lord, through your son, Jesus, for this gift of writing.

To my parents, Mr. Salvador Oledan and the late Mrs. Patrocenia de Lara Oledan. Your upbringing made me the best that I can be.

To my sister, Socorro O. Brazil and brother, Edgardo Oledan, and their families for being the most supportive siblings I could have ever known.

To my husband, Ferdinand: the wind beneath my wings.

To Mr. Rodante Guardia, for the wonderful illustrations.

To Ms. Heather Linday, for her very kind help editing.

To Ms. Donna Rivera of Elite Printing for giving me the idea to publish a book on Saipan.

To the hemodialysis care providers of the Commonwealth Health Center for demonstrating the true meaning of friendship.

Special thanks to author and coach, Walt F.J. Goodridge, for his kind assistance in the design, layout and publication of this book, and without whose help, this book may not be in physical form.

To all the nice people of Saipan, and the Commonwealth of the Northern Mariana Islands.

And to my son, Eman Ramos for pushing me to work harder and to dream bigger!

www.ingramcontent.com/pod-product-compliance
Lightning Source LLC
LaVergne TN
LVHW010025070426
835509LV00001B/19